She Who Cried Wolf

Alexis Stillgess

BookLeaf Publishing

India | USA | UK

Presentation by *BookLeaf Publishing*

Web: www.bookleafpub.com

E-mail: info@bookleafpub.com

ISBN: 9789358735581

First edition 2023

*To all of the people who feel as though they
are alone in their deepest feelings and
darkest thoughts throughout life -*

*You are not alone. You can battle your
demons one day at a time.*

ACKNOWLEDGEMENT

I would like to acknowledge all of the friends and family encouraging me to write since I was a child. Thank you to my parents who raised me as they did, and to my siblings for sticking around me long enough. Thank you to my friends who do not hold back their criticism. Thank you to the people who caused me to feel such emotions that have been expressed by this book. You were truly an inspiration. Thank you especially to the friends that have stuck around long enough to see me make it this far.

I would also like to acknowledge my son. Little Tyler Aiden. You make me feel like I can breathe again. Aside from the darkness in this book, you have come to make my world light. I will forever love you to the ends of the universe. If you ever experience any cruelty from this world we call life, just know that you are never alone.

Beauty

My eyes aren't blue.
They can't compare with the beautiful ocean
depths infused with its coral beauties.
They can't swallow you up and make you lost
like when you look into an endless sea.
They can't change colors or even cloud your
vision like the sky.

My eyes aren't green.
They can't make you feel curious like you're
looking into the forest.
They can't remind you of some marvelous
adventure to an emerald city.
They're not multicolored when the light hits
them just right like a beautiful gemstone.

My hair isn't long.
It isn't blonde or ombré.
It isn't curly or even perfectly straight.

My skin isn't flawless.
I have a birthmark. An odd spot.
I have freckles all over my body.
I have scars.

Not just on my legs or my arms, but also on my
face and in my mind.
I have mental and physical scars.
I have stretch marks.

My face is asymmetrical.
My smile isn't perfect.
But
I don't wear a mask.

My eyes are brown.
They aren't blue, green, or even hazel.
They're brown like the mud in the ground.
Brown like the bark on the trees.
And in the shining daylight,
They are golden like the sun.
Golden like the honey you pour in your tea.
They are treasure, hidden in plain sight.

My hair is brown.
It's short.
It isn't perfect, it has split ends and dead ends.
And even though it isn't straight or curly,
It's wild like life itself.

My skin isn't flawless.
It has marks.
It isn't clean.
It isn't beautiful.

But it's natural, and it tells a story.
My story.

Beauty.
a combination of qualities, such as shape, color,
or form, that pleases the aesthetic senses,
especially the sight.

Beauty.
It's a matter of differing opinions.

You say that I am beautiful, like a butterfly.
But if I told you that I was a moth instead of a
butterfly,
Would you still say that I am so?

Words Left Unsaid

Hey,

Yeah?

You're great.

No I'm not.

Yes you are.

I hate you.

You're great.

Why are you talking to me..

You're great.

Why do you keep saying that?

So I don't say anything else.

Because you just are.

You're great.

I miss you.. I miss you so damn much.

You're great.

So are you.

I love you.

You're great.

You're great too, you really are.

Why am I still responding..

You're great

Why are you saying that? Do we need to
FaceTime?

Please.. I really want to.. I can't stop crying. I
miss you. I love you. And this isn't fair.

No we don't need to FaceTime, I just wanted to
say that. You're great.

You've hurt me so much.

You're great.

Well in case you didn't know, you're greater
than great.

But still not good enough for you..

No I didn't know, but thank you.

What am I doing wrong..

You're great.

So you have a girlfriend..

That's great.

You're great.

What do you want from me. Why are you
literally still talking to me.

You're great.

I care about you. You're great too.

Haha.. right.. I care about you. Me?
You care about me?

You are great.

I wish I could just stop loving you.

You are great.

I don't know what to say to you anymore.. and
yet there's so much I want to say.

Don't say it
Don't say it.
Don't say it.
Don't say it.

I..

Yes?

You're great.*

I miss you.

You're great.

I don't trust you anymore..

You're great.

I'm glad you're doing just fine.

You're great.

I love you.

You're great.

Stop saying that

Why?

………..
You're great..

Monster under the Bed

"I'm the same little girl that believes monsters
are just misunderstood."

Misunderstood. Misunderstood?
.....
is that what you are?

He looks at her with innocent eyes.

You are a monster, but are you just that?

He watches her.

Misunderstood.
Like a definition.

"a declaration or assurance that one will do a
particular thing or that a particular thing will
happen."

Misunderstood.

She turns her back to him and he smirks.

Like a promise.

"I promise I'm different."

Different?

I believe you.

A wide grin spreads across his face as he quietly approaches her with fangs flashing.

"I promised I've changed."

I trust you.

This is it. He's almost on top of her.

"I promise I love you."

I love you too..

'That's it. Now just to rip her heart to shreds and
eat it.'
He's right there.
But just as she turns back to him, he's instantly
back to his normal innocent facade.

I love you too.
She says with tears rushing down her face.

You are just misunderstood.

She hugs him tightly, and he tenses up just a bit.
His predatory instincts rise up. He hesitates.
Instead of ripping her to shreds, he wraps his
arms around her. He was surprised.

"I guess little girls are misunderstood too."

First Real Heartbreak

I can't sleep
I'm so tired.
I am so fucking tired
But it doesn't matter what I try,
I just can't sleep...
At least.. not with you on my mind.
You texted me.
"It's hard sleeping not knowing how you are
doing, how are you holding up??"
I should have responded with
"I can't relate."
And then turned and went to sleep,
But we both know I carried on the conversation.
You text me knowing I'll respond every single
time.
But then you say you don't want to talk to me.
You call me to say that you miss me and that you
love me.
Then you leave, and you say you don't want to
be together.
You say I'm sorry.
I'm sorry?
"I'm sorry I was trying to fight with you on
purpose so you would leave me. I really am

thankful for you, you are way stronger than you think Alexis"
You say I'm way stronger than I think, but you continue to walk all over me because you know you can. You say I'm strong, but you know I'm weak when it comes to you. It's like Batman telling Superman he's strong, and then throwing kryptonite in his face.
As corny as it is, you are my kryptonite.
No.
You were my kryptonite.
Were.
Now you're just an unhealthy drug.
Toxically intoxicating.
A parasite.
A mistletoe.
Not the one you kiss under, but the one that kills slowly but surely.
Better yet.
With every word.
Look.
Touch.
Embrace.
With every kiss.
You took away all of me. Slowly. But surely
All of me.
And just like the giving tree, I gave everything away without hesitation.

You took everything, and left me a stump. And
then still came back for more.
And while I have nothing more to give, I'm still
here for you. Trying to give.
But why?
Because I care for you.
I love you.

I hate you. I love you, and I hate that I want you.

But just like my energy and motivation to keep
going, my want for you is slowly starting to
fade.

I still just can't seem to let you go.
Like a child with a teddy bear.
She turned 21 today, and even though she knows
she doesn't need that teddy bear anymore she
just can't seem to let it go.
I can't let you go.

 I. can't. sleep.
At least, not with you on my mind.

I could lie, and I could say that I could.
I could try, and I could say that I did.
I could continue to smile and say:
I'm okay. I'm not tired. I'm wide awake.

"Fake it till you make it, right?"
But am I really making it if I'm just constantly
faking it?

Suffocating

This is ridiculous.
Waiting for words to prove how I'm feeling
Which can easily be explained by watching the
ceiling.
You must admit, the anticipation has got to be
pretty scary
While I sit here and try to improve on my
vocabulary.
And it's so freaking absurd.
The power of that one word…
Love.
Loss.
Heartbreak.
No.

It's 3:33 in the morning and I'm laying here
alone.
Obviously not sleeping. Not crying or creeping.
Not eating. Not seeing. Not blinking. Not
breathing.
Not breathing? Oh god.

Here we go again.
With the writing and repeating
About this depression that's defeating

These words that are deafening
And these drugs that are beckoning.
Saying that I'm suffocating
When really I'm just complicating
All of these words that I'm not saying..

Fifty Shades

Fifty shades of grey? More like fifty shades
darker.
Fifty shards of glass? Try fifty times sharper.
It was lust that was lost.
And our trust is now gone.

The Act

19

Sex.
It isn't inspiration, it's pleasure.
An act of desire with passion like burning fire.
Wearing my skin like fashionable attire
And hiding behind my clothes like barbed wire.

Confession.

20

Temptation.
More than just a word, it's an urge.
Taking the action and confusing it with passion.
And you gain a life lesson
With that one accused confession.

Temptation.

Fingers in his hair because I like how it feels.
He smirks with a wink and he's giving me chills.
He said he cut his hair and I told him I liked it,
his smile grew wide and he got so excited

I leaned in closer and bent his will to give in,
I wanted it. I needed it. That passionate sin..

Oh man just tease, just a taste
Needless to say both our hearts raced

As he got closer
Still running my fingers through his hair over
and over
Feet turned to inches as we were closing that
distance
Thoughts racing through my mind about this one
little instance

I got too excited
And it was getting hard to hide it

Inches turned to centimeters and
My skin was on fire
There was nothing more that I wanted
Just that one desire.

Desperation -

22

I'm lying in bed, but I'm high as a kite
I know it's one in the morning, but it feels so
right.
I'm thinking about you and I'm thinking about
cake
Amazing smell
Looks fucking fantastic
So warm..
Rich
Sweet..
Just one bite… one taste..
Of the cake of course.

Alright alright -
Stop tugging at my sleeve
I can feel your anticipation,
And it's given me a bit of inspiration.

I'm trapped.
Trapped in my head as I'm sinking into this bed
Trapped in my mind
It's almost like I'm blind
Like seeing what it's like to not see for the first
time.

I know the words are there, but I can't tell you
what they are.
I can only describe how they feel…
Loud..
Lustful..
Intoxicating..
Just one look into those eyes and..
Sorry I'm getting off topic, so unbecoming of
me,
I know.

So I started this job, and I'm kind of really new.
It's early in the morning in a happy atmosphere,
But then there was you.
Just a bit groggy and foggy, going on this
pessimistic spree,
Which stopped the moment I turned and said
"Hi, my name is Lexie"
You introduced yourself, and apologized for that
first impression.
Personally I thought it was a cute little rant
session.

Of course things evolved.
A conversation to a joke
A meal to a movie
Short days to long nights.
And now you're just missing all of the things
that I'm not saying.

Now it's three in the morning, and I'm clearly
still awake.
Definitely thinking of you, and not about cake.
But now I'm back to the words that are stuck in
my mind.
These words I can only feel because I've
become so blind.

Gentle
That feeling when your fingers are in my hair
When your hands are tracing my skin
Or rubbing my shoulders at the end of the day.
That look you give when hearing about bad
times.

Loud
My thoughts when we're alone.
Your breathing in my ear.
Your heartbeat when I'm around.

Intoxicating
That look in your eyes as they turn darker
colors.
Your touch
Your smell
Your "just one kiss?"

Lustful

When you're pinning me down
Staring into my eyes as you make me feel
helpless
When those soft rubs become rough grabs
When you bite down and the world just melts
away..

Desperate
I'm desperate.
Desperate for that look you make.
Desperate for the touch of your skin.
I'm desperate for that kiss.
Well..
I guess you could just say that
I'm desperate for this.

Cassandra -

To my sister-

Remember the times when people thought we were twins?
And then things switched up, and nobody thought we were kin.
They'd ask if we had different parents, like it was a sin.
But we were one in the same, like a pencil and pen.

Remember the time I started school without you?
I cried that first day at kindergarten, because I was afraid to be alone.
For the next two years I'd spend my days there, and you'd spend your days home.

Remember the time there, when I was being bullied by everyone.
No one came to my rescue, and back then I was alone.
Then you showed up and punched Michael Brown in his chest,
And from that day on, he called you the devil.

But you were my hero.

Remember the time when mom and dad got into
their first real fight?
It was at Ethan's house, pretty late at night.
They came in drunk, and fighting, and they
woke everyone up.
All the kids were in tears until the cops showed
up.
This was one of the first times I realized I was
the oldest,
And I wanted nothing more than to protect you.

Remember the time Xavier almost killed you?
You came running into the room crying and
begging for me to save you.
I shoved him back, and shut his face in the door.
But it slammed back open, and I thought he
wanted more.
It was actually dad coming in to say that if you
want to start something you finish it.
I hated him for saying that, but I promised
myself if you guys ever got in another fight
I wouldn't let you finish it.
I'd finish it for you.

To my Sister -
We grew up fighting, but we grew up close.
Lately it has just felt as though we're estranged.

I love you to no end, and I never want you to
leave.
I will fight with you, I will fight by you, and I
will fight for you.
Even when it seems I am far away, I am always
with you.
I love you.

In the Dark.

29

Left alone with these suicidal thoughts
In this world like fluttering moths
Scuttling close to get to that flame
Turning to dust with nothing but
Shame.

Behind these Eyes.

I'm smiling in the mirror
And what do I see?
Of course it's my reflection
Staring right back at me.

The animation I'm watching
Is a sight for sore eyes.
There's three copies of Me
Hidden behind all these lies.

The first one is anxious
She's scratching at her skin
She's shaking up the glass
Trying to find a way to get in.

Her hair is frazzled,
And her eyes are wide.
She's hyperventilating and stuttering
Looking for a guide.

The second one is depressed
And I haven't got a clue,
But it looks like she's crying
And she's breaking over you.

She's hysterical and in tears
She's shattered at her core
She cannot even fathom
Why you ever called her 'Whore'

The third one is laughing.
Maniacal psycho is her name.
She's from a special kind of hell
And torture is her game.

Any damage that you've done,
She deals back tenfold.
She will peel off your skin
Then leave you in the cold.

What I see in my reflection,
Is what I must hide.
I tell you I'm okay,
And I know that I've lied.

The Truth is I'm alive.
And I'm kind of really sad.
I am really fucking angry.
But I'm also really glad.

Accidental Suicide -

The reaper has come
And has presented a choice
I shake my head no
Because I can't find my voice

There's a girl in the bath
Holding a needle and thread
But you can't fix a mistake
When you're already dead.

The reaper is waiting
As my memories cloud my eyes
I still cannot answer
As I watch my own demise

I really messed up
I should've stayed around
How long will it take
Until I'll be found?

Surely I can fix this.
There has to be way
I nod to the reaper
I do want to stay

I'm delusional at this point.
The panic has set in
How could I do this?
The ultimate sin

I'm touching my body
What can I do?
Cover myself
In staples and glue?

That should keep my soul in place
Long enough to heal
My heart should restart
Aiding me to feel

My talent is to please
The people who are around
This mistake should be fixed
Before my corpse is found

The reaper is watching me
As I lay in my bed
I snuggle up in my pillows
Feeling nothing but dread

What else can I do
To fix this mistake
I'm already laying here
Staying awake

I just thought about it,
and I haven't eaten today.
Do you think an apple
would still keep the doctor away?

Vulnerability

To the person who once said, "you're afraid of
commitment." -

Maybe you were right.
Maybe I am afraid.

I'm afraid to talk.
I'm afraid to breathe.
I'm afraid to connect.
I'm afraid to forget.

I'm afraid to walk in new places.
I'm afraid to chart unknown territories.
I'm afraid of breaking down my walls.
I'm afraid of others watching me fall.

I'm afraid of losing my filters.
I'm afraid to speak my mind.
I'm afraid of taking a stand.
I'm afraid of making a plan.

I'm afraid to feel.
I'm afraid of getting hurt.
I'm afraid of being rejected,
And I'm afraid of being accepted.

I'm afraid to cry,
And I'm afraid to die.
But I'm afraid to live,
And I'm even more afraid to try.

I'm afraid of letting go
I'm afraid of following through.
I'm afraid of letting things be.
Realistically, I'm just afraid to be me.

So to this person who said this to me years ago -

You left a scared scar on my heart, but maybe
you were wrong.

I'm not afraid of commitment.

I'm afraid of being vulnerable.

I Am Sad!

37

Because saying I am sad isn't enough.

I AM SAD.
I am sad.

I am screaming and nobody hears me.
I am drowning and nobody sees me.
I am dying and nobody is saving me.

I'm tired of moving.
I'm tired of people leaving.
I'm tired of being lost
And feeling unsafe.

I'm tired of uncertainty.
I'm tired of insecurities.
I'm tired of being built up
Just to be torn down.

I'm tired of trying to find my way home
When I don't have one.

I'm tired of wiping my tears.
I'm tired of being here.

And then there was You.

38

Now I'm back to the words stuck in my mind.
 These words I can only feel because I've
become so blind.
 Feel the warmth on my skin and into my core.
Running vivid colors through the sky I can feel
from your sun that shines.

To My Sunshine

Breaking free from dependency,
I found my wings to soar, so free.
Love's embrace, my soul does leap,
With the one who takes my heart to keep.

No longer chained, I rise above,
In his warm glow, I found true love.
Happiness blooms like flowers in spring,
With you, my love, my everything.

In your arms, I find my sanctuary,
With you, love shines, like rays so bright.
You're my sunshine, my heart's luminary,
Guiding me through each day and night.

In your presence, I feel so secure,
A love that's steadfast, forever intact.
From Earth to Moon, my love is pure,
To the moon and back, that's a loving fact.

Lost

"Walkin hella fast to class with these flash shoes
from the past"
You come from the future, and I come from the
past. Maybe that's why we just aren't meant to
last. Just sitting here in the present is making me
feel so hesitant..
I've become so lost..
Lost..

____

Lost in the sauce boss

____

Lost more so than ever before
Walked through that door only to be called a
whore
I wanted a fresh start
But all I got was a broken heart
You brainwashed me into thinking you were my
new dream
While you sat behind the curtains ripping my
every seam.

Late Night.

It's four o'clock in the morning,
And my body is having a race.
My heart is pumping eagerly
And my mind isn't struggling to
Keep up the pace.

My blood is coursing
Through my body
While these thoughts
Are forcing me awake
Can this be reality
Or can this just be fake.

Fake or real
Real or fake
As if I had a choice.
Make one wrong decision
And my whole life is at stake.

Why am I doing this
Why am I doing that
Should I keep this dog
Or should I get a cat

Why didn't I say this

Why couldn't I do that
Why do I still feel this way
Why do I still look back

Yes
No
Maybe
So

How can everything feel so wrong
But somehow manage to still be right

Premeditated Break-Up

My hands are empty,
They're icy and cold.
Because I no longer have
Your hands to hold.

My skin is burning
For the warmth of your embrace.
My eyes are searching
For the sight of your face.

My fingers are feeling
For your tousled hair.
My mind is reeling
Into a pit of despair.

I'm crying out
And screaming your name
My soul is searching
Trying to find yours in vain

I'm on my knees
And gasping for air.
My mind can't process
How this could be fair.

You were surrounded by light
When you came into my life.
You told me you loved me,
Almost made me your wife.

Then you grew bored.
You left as quickly as you came.
You took away my sunshine,
Left me with nothing but shame.

Now my being is left empty
After my soul has been sold.
You took your warmth away
And left me icy and cold.